Turner and the Channel

This exhibition is sponsored by

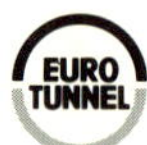

Turner and the Channel
THEMES AND VARIATIONS c.1845

The Tate Gallery

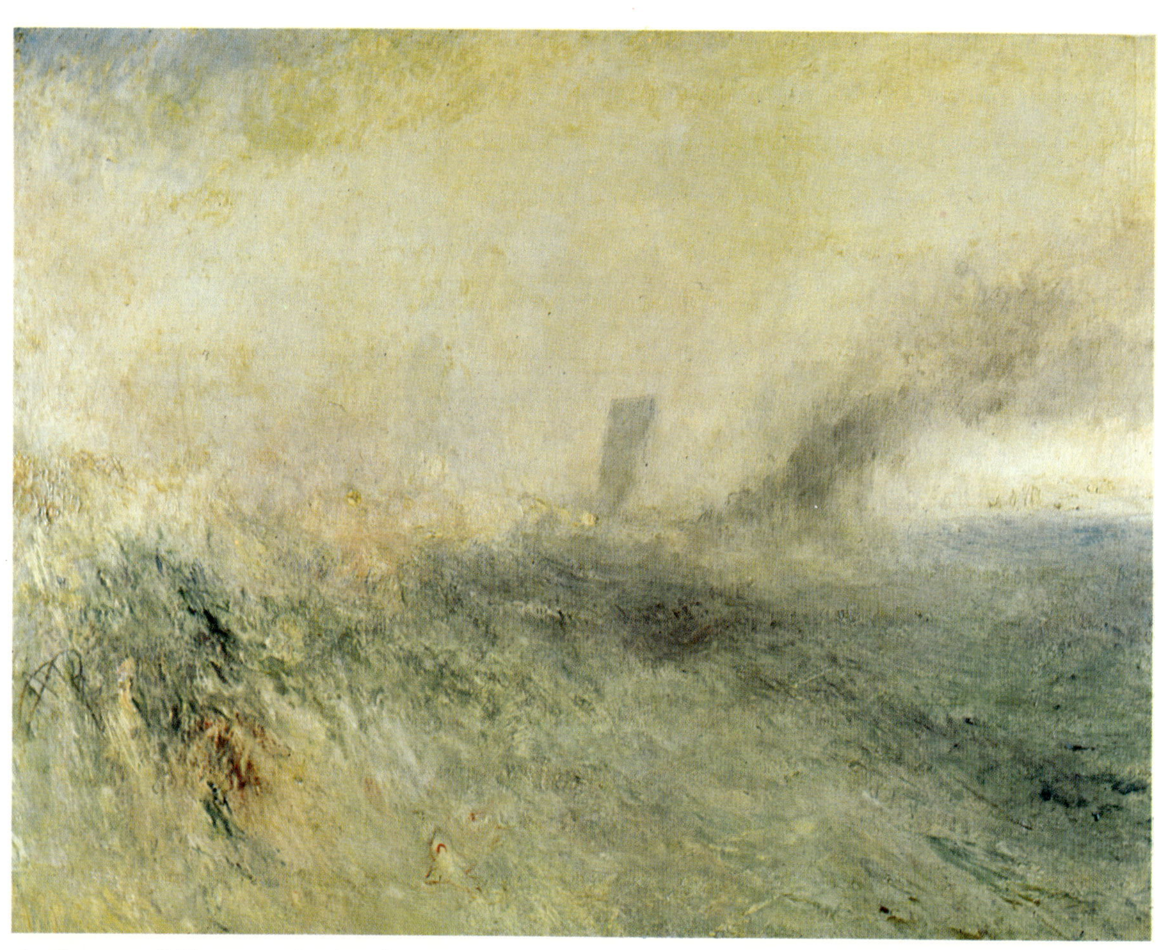

pl.1 **Seascape: Folkestone** _c._1845 (cat.1)

Foreword

As the permanent home of the nation's collection of Turner's work the Clore Gallery is a natural setting for temporary exhibitions dealing with different aspects of his output, his life and his times. Although these will draw primarily on material in the Turner Bequest, they will also from time to time incorporate loans from elsewhere. Indeed, it is to be hoped that the Gallery will come to be thought of as the logical and proper place for the public display of works by Turner from many different sources.

The first of these special exhibitions is *Turner and the Channel: Themes and Variations*. It concentrates on his work along the Picardy and Kent coasts in the mid-1840s. An exploration of this little-discussed and elusive subject has been prompted by two generous and very significant loans from private collectors: the canvas known as *Folkestone*, formerly in the collection of Lord Clark, and the small 'Channel' sketchbook which resurfaced last year and was sold at auction in London. Both attracted great interest and fetched large sums, the Clark picture breaking all previous auction records for an oil painting. The sketchbook is a unique object in being the only important example of an intact book of studies by Turner to survive outside the Turner Bequest.

We are very pleased to be able to salute these two distinguished items, and to give them an opportunity to shed their particular light on that part of the collection to which, as illustrations of Turner's working methods, they both in a sense belong. We extend our warmest thanks to their owners for making the exhibition possible, and are grateful to various people for their help in preparing it: Evelyn Joll, Sue Valentine and Henry Wemyss in particular. David Blayney Brown, Assistant Keeper in the Turner Collection at the Tate Gallery, has selected and catalogued the exhibits, and has written the introduction to the catalogue.

Alan Bowness *Director*

Turner and the Channel:
Themes and Variations *c*.1845

A surge of sea, a rising wave sweeping some small creatures up from the depths to cast them before us in a cascade of foam; beyond it the hint of a ship, a small steamer probably, trailing a dark parabola of smoke from its stack; beyond this the calmer waters of a coastline, shimmering blue, and a glimpse of cliffs in sunshine; these are home waters, rough enough to disturb a landsman but, for Turner, a familiar and habitable element. Turner's 'Seascape; Folkestone', of about 1845 (Cat.1, pl.1), speaks to us on a note of affirmation and celebration. Long experience and observation has enabled him to enter the very substance of the sea, to conjure its internal and organic life. The alienation of the apocalyptic Sublime seems far away.

It is not at all certain that this picture has much to do with Folkestone. We can, however, be fairly sure that it is set somewhere in the Channel, and dates from around 1845. The former title, 'Storm off the Foreland', may be the more accurate. The present name arises from an association, first made in 1960, with a type of study to be found in the 'Folkestone' and 'Dieppe' sketchbooks (Cat. 25 & 22), although in fact there are closer parallels elsewhere in the drawings of 1845, notably in the final sheet of the 'Ambleteuse and Wimereux' book used that spring (Cat. 17). The wider stylistic arguments for placing the picture about this year have been discussed by Butlin and Joll, who note the bright colour, with a predominance of green, as a feature shared with oils of 1844.[1] However, the peculiarly iridescent quality of the paint, and the lightness of touch, are hard to match at all and in many respects the picture stands alone.

The date and identity of the work have been obscured by the absence of any provenance before 1894 when it was in the possession of an important collector of Turner, Sir Donald Currie. There are strong similarities to the late canvases that stem from Mrs Booth, Turner's mistress and companion in later years firstly in Margate and later in Chelsea, and from her son by her first marriage, John Pound.[2] Although more probably disposed of by Turner himself to one of his last patrons like Joseph Gillott or Elhanan Bicknell – which would imply that Turner thought of it as finished – the picture is sufficiently close to the Booth items to justify further investigation of Turner's work at Margate and along the Channel coast in the 1840s. Moreover, the other most important single item in this exhibition, the 'Channel' sketchbook of *c*1845 (Cat. 8, pls. 2-5), may confidently be traced to a Booth source. Both picture and sketchbook arose from one of Turner's more sustained activities in the last years of his life – the study of the seas, sands and skies of Kent and the Channel that is the theme of this exhibition.

Turner and Margate

That Turner's favourite haunt on the Kent coast was not properly on the Channel at all, but Margate on the North Foreland, was mainly due to Mrs Booth. Thornbury, in one of his contentious stories, suggests an older attachment, claiming that Turner was sent at the age of thirteen to school at Margate where he 'first saw the sea' and 'learnt the physiognomy of the waves'.[3] In fact Turner had been there even earlier, in about 1786, to stay with relatives of his mother; his first views of the town were made in his tenth year and one (private collection) contains his earliest depiction of sea-going ships.[4] Another story tells of a youthful love affair in Margate. Be this as it may, Turner was certainly a regular visitor to Mrs Booth by the late 1820s.

Sophia Caroline Booth settled in Margate in 1827 with her second husband. Widowed in 1833, she readily formed a relationship with Turner who had taken lodgings in her house for summer visits, and she continued to receive him frequently until, in 1846, she came to keep house for him in

pls 2–5 **'Channel' Sketchbook** c.1845 (cat.8)

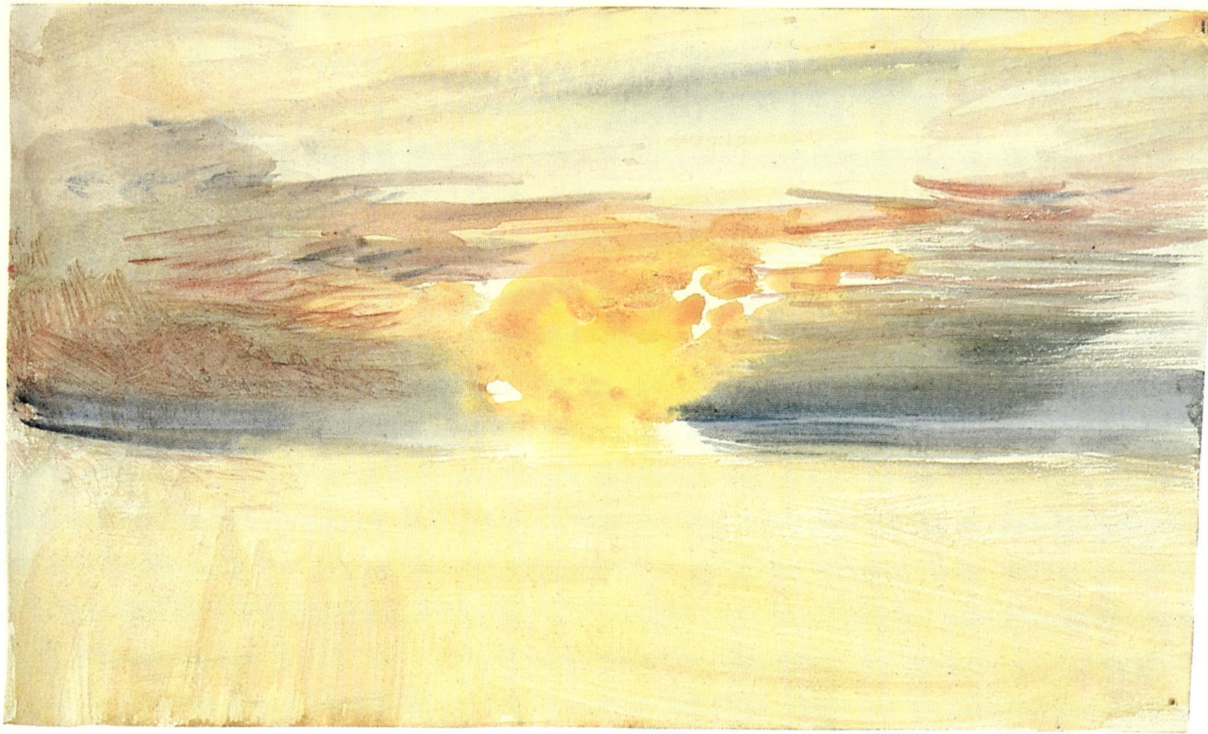

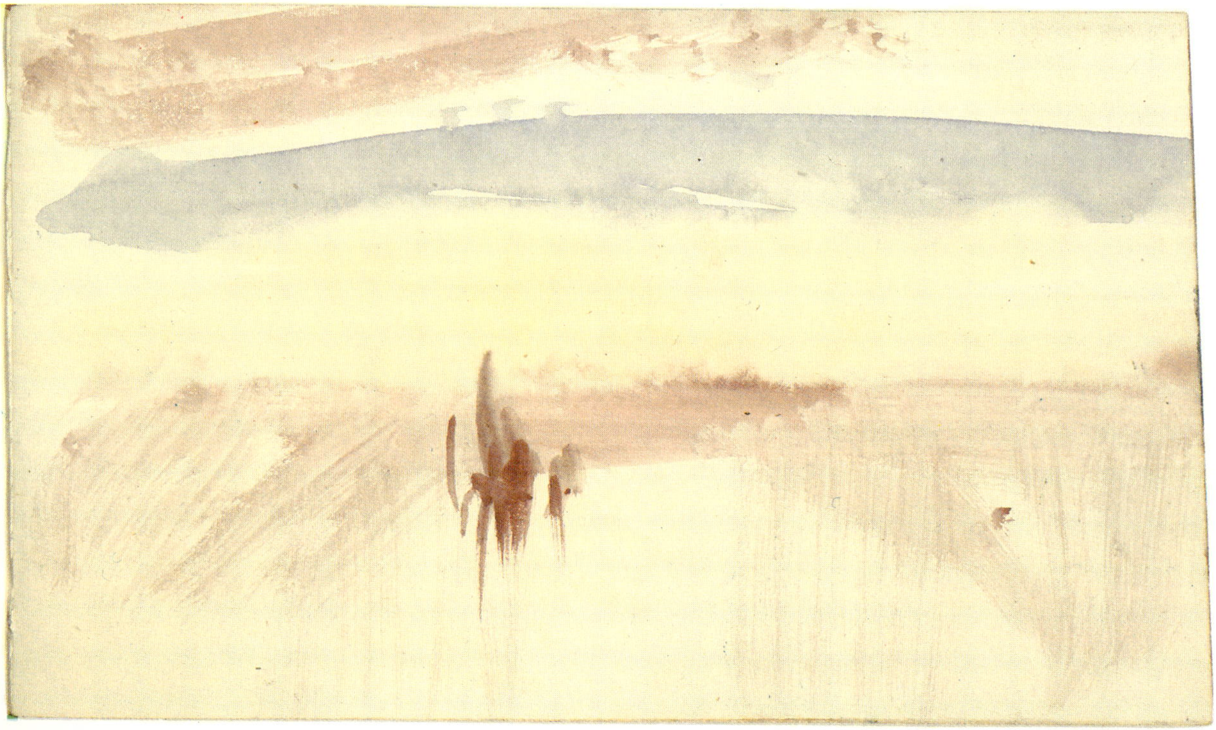

pl.3

[8]

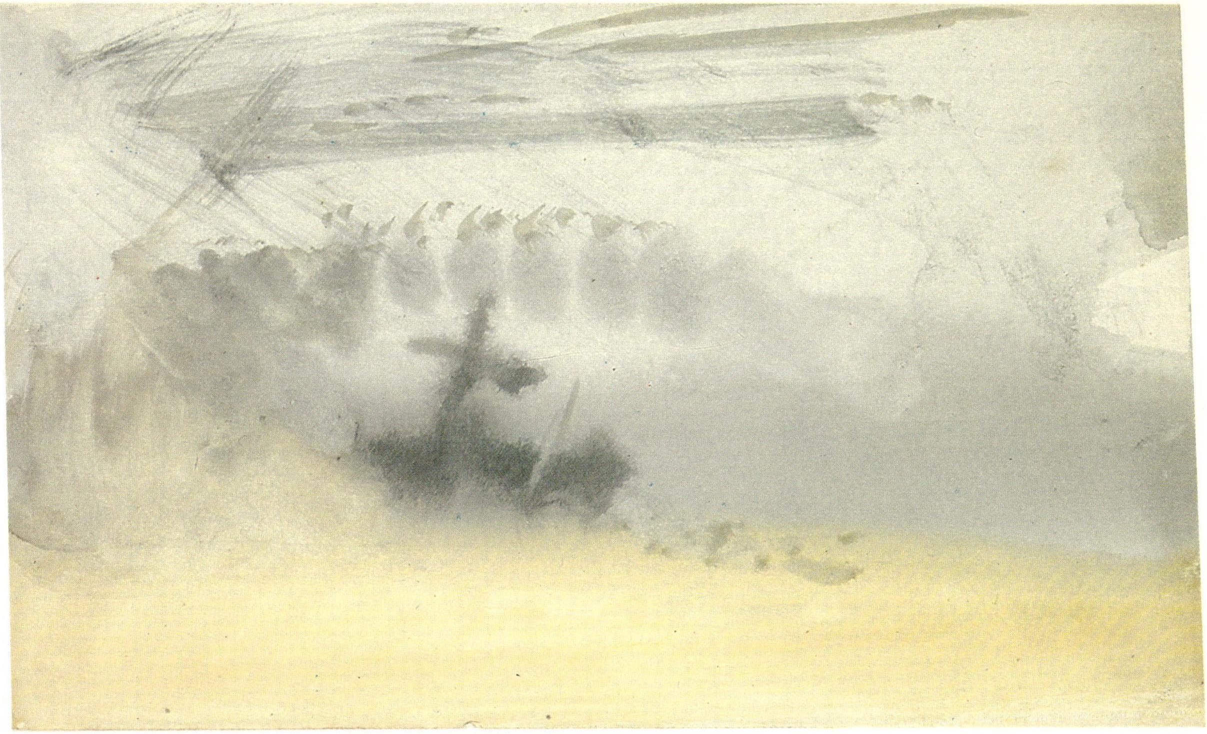

pl.4

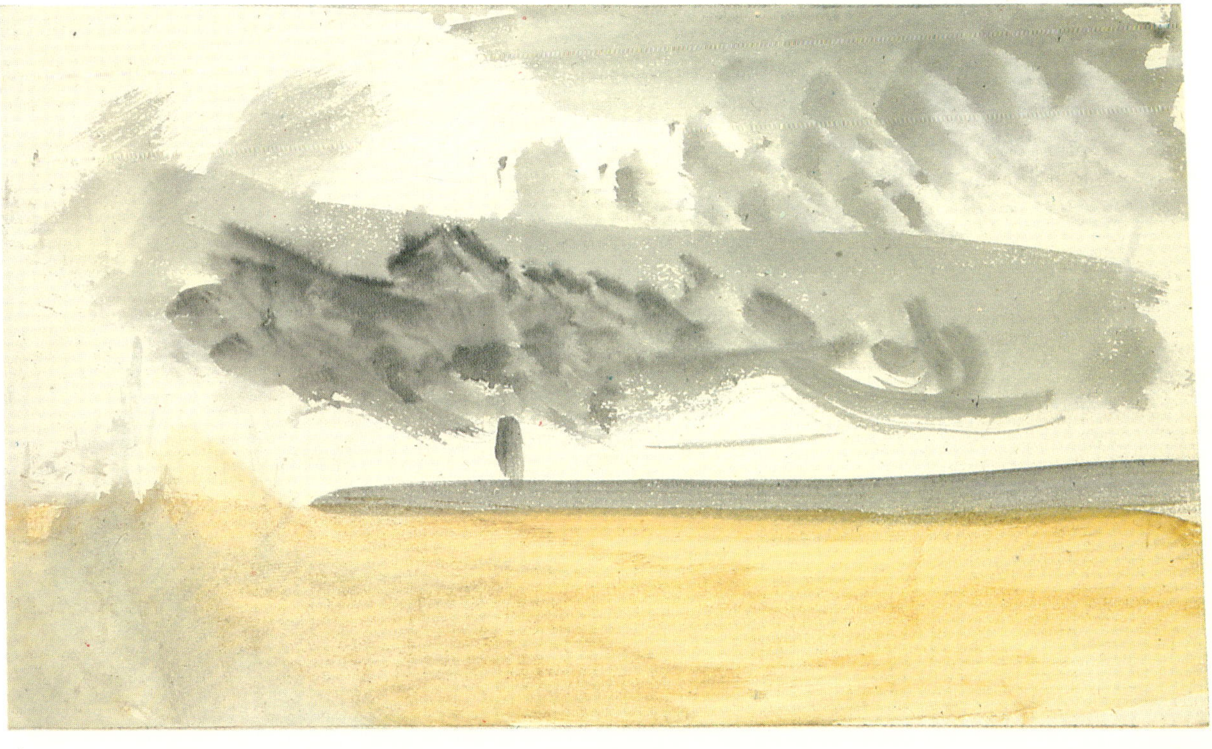

pl.5

London. Turner was characteristically secretive about his visits to Mrs Booth, but it is clear that they played an important part in his life, being both emotionally sustaining and artistically productive. His trips to Margate must have had the air of holidays while being easily made from London, for there were already regular steamer services from London Bridge Wharf to Herne Bay and Margate three times a week; Turner preferred the Saturday boat, and must often have stayed for much longer than a weekend.

The passenger steamers were soon to transform the town and within thirty years it would be hard to recall the charms of Turner's Margate. Introducing Turner's view, as engraved by Thomas Lupton for *The Harbours of England* published in 1856, Ruskin thought it 'very notably capricious' of his hero to devote such sustained attention to so prosaic a town, for 'Margate is simply a mass of modern parades and streets, with a little bit of chalk cliff, an orderly pier, and some bathing machines'. By 1871 things had deteriorated and Ruskin could cull some horrified letters from *The Times* like this one from 'C.L.S.':

> SIR,—On Monday last I had the misfortune of taking a trip per steamer to Margate. The sea was rough, the ship crowded, and therefore most of the Cockney excursionists prostrate with sea-sickness. On landing on Margate Pier I must confess I thought that, instead of landing in an English sea port, I had been transported by magic to a land inhabited by savages and lunatics.

Others complained of indecent bathing, and the 'hopeless, hideous din' that prevailed in the streets during the season. Now, however, further to dramatise this picture of English decadence for the members of the Guild of St George, Ruskin painted a pleasanter picture of the Margate of his own youth, when it was much as Turner knew it – a bow-fronted inn with a print or two of a revenue cutter and the Battle of the Nile, a bowl of fresh shrimps and wonderful air – and recalled Turner's praise for the beautiful skies of the town and its hinterland of 'corn-bearing chalk';

He knew the colours of the clouds over the sea, from the Bay of Naples to the Hebrides; and being once asked where, in Europe, were to be seen the loveliest skies, answered instantly, 'In the Isle of Thanet'. Where, therefore, and in this very town of Margate, he lived, when he chose to be quit of London, and yet not to travel.[5]

Margate, with its beach, breakwater and pier, was an interesting enough subject in itself. Turner's most considered views of it are of course those that served for engraving, the rather similar views from the sea in the *Southern Coast* and *The Harbours of England*, and that looking down into the town from high ground in *Picturesque Views of England and Wales* (Cat. 50). Its more intimate bustle can be imagined from the delightful sketches in the 'Gravesend and Margate' sketchbook used on a visit in about 1832 (Cat. 9); the harbour and beach, local trades and characters, are caught in great variety in a sequence of swift pencil sketches. Mrs Booth's house, a small one next to the Custom House and the Foy Boat Inn, overlooking Cold Harbour, provided Turner with an excellent vantage point, and his view, of the beach and breakwater with the pier on the left, may be recognized in various sketches in the Bequest (Cat. 29 & 43 fig. 10).[6] Margate was also a convenient point of departure for the Kent coast as a whole and sketchbooks provide evidence of his travels along the shore, sometimes drawing from a boat. His chief concern, however, was with the changing moods of sea and sky, and he needed to go no further than his Margate window to observe them in all the variety that attracted him to other favourite and familiar subjects like Venice or Mont Rigi.

The large numbers of studies, in oil as well as in watercolours, of beaches, breaking waves, and coastal shipping from the 1830s and early 40s must owe much to Margate and Mrs Booth. There are quantities of late marine studies in the Bequest, but of the quite finished oils, a group outside it is most relevant to this discussion. Since most of these pictures devolved to Mrs Booth, it is reasonable to assume that they were painted in her house. Most originally had Margate titles in the Pound sale in 1862, and while these can have been little more than guesswork, they probably expressed the essential truth. These oils might be divided into two categories. Firstly there are quite developed pictures with a strong narrative or figural content and a somewhat melancholy atmosphere. Examples are the 'Margate Harbour' (Butlin & Joll 475) at Sudley Hall, Liverpool, 'Wreckers on the Coast; Sun rising through Mist' (Butlin & Joll 477) in a German private collection, and 'Morning after the Wreck' (Butlin & Joll 478) in the National Museum of Wales. Secondly one might turn to sketches or less worked pictures that are more preoccupied with the sea itself, stormier in effect, and more abstract in composition, such as the two canvases in the Yale Center for British Art, 'Off the Nore; Wind and Water' (Butlin & Joll 476) and 'Waves breaking on the Shore' (Butlin & Joll 482), 'Off Ramsgate?' (Butlin & Joll 479) in an American Collection, and 'Off Deal' (Butlin & Joll 483) in the Nationalmuseum, Stockholm. The titles and dates of these oils have been much debated, and at least one critic, Luke Herrmann, has questioned the attribution in several cases, but it is to these works, as much as any in the Bequest, that we must look to assemble the background for 'Seascape; Folkestone'.

These 'Booth' pictures are consistently small, while 'Folkestone' is of Turner's standard 3ft by 4ft size, matched, for late coast sketches, mainly in the Bequest. A sequence of these large oils in the Bequest runs a gamut of colour and effect from the vivid blaze and saturated handling of 'Stormy Sea with Dolphins' (Butlin & Joll 463) to the cold greens and greys, and crisp, striated brushwork of 'Rough Sea' (Cat. 2). Among the most developed of these, although by no means finished, are the so-called 'Margate' (Butlin & Joll 464) in the National Gallery, and the 'Sunrise with Sea Monsters' (Cat. 3), those ambiguous works in the first of which Turner has introduced what may be the prow of an antique ship or the tail of a leaping fish, and in the second fantastic creatures of the deep. In both cases his fecund imagination plays on subjects long familiar, much as it does in 'Folkestone' where the composition is still more fully wrought and the waves are made pregnant with life.

There are, besides, some four oils in the Bequest which treat of stormy seas and breaking waves in a richer palette of blue, yellow and green and are generally dated to the 1830s. Turner's interest in waves was of course not new – it can be traced back to some of his earliest drawings – but must have been stimulated afresh during the years that he visited Margate. Counterparts for these oil studies can be found in various drawings, notably in a small group in bodycolours on blue paper that clearly belong to a sequence and attest to systematic study of the action of the seas (ie. Cat. 30 & 31), and in the equally strong drawings of beach scenes, this time on a buff preparation, that have been convincingly reassembled by Edward Yardley as the contents of a Margate sketchbook of about 1835-40.[7] All these sheets are marked by powerful and positive effects, and by the juxtaposition of coloured grounds with strong, dry bodycolour, that are to be found in Petworth and Venetian drawings of that period. Apart from their robust technique, there is little evidence for dating either the oils or the drawings. It is sufficient to imagine Turner, at Mrs Booth's window or on the beach at Margate, Deal or Folkestone, exploring the effects he had always loved and would return to in the 1840s when advancing age made travel further afield more exiguous.

The material assembled for discussion here is offered, with varying degrees of certainty, as characteristic of Turner's Kent and Channel studies in the middle of that decade. With the drawings of 1845 itself, one is on fairly sure ground for Turner's activities are well documented and his sketchbooks, whose leaves are sometimes dated, provide a standard of comparison. For the rest, one must be guided mainly by eye. Sheets have been drawn from the Bequest – most often from those manifold and still mysterious riches labelled by Finberg as 'MISCELLANEOUS: COLOUR' – because they seem to fall into categories of subject and technique that are anticipated or comprehended by the dated sketchbooks, or by the 'Channel' book which all the evidence indicates is also of 1845. The drawings, in turn, invite comparison with the late oil sketches of coastal subjects rediscovered in the early 1960s. Cataloguing these, Butlin and Joll dauntingly declared that 'compositional resemblances help very little in dating Turner's late works and comparison between works in different media is equally fruitless'. This exhibition is unashamedly based on such comparisons, the object being to illuminate trends in Turner's late work – especially in his approach to certain types of subject matter – rather than to fix it to any precise time or place.

Turner in 1845

1845 proved a most taxing year for Turner. He exhibited six pictures at the Royal Academy, and was serving on the Academy council, standing in at the meetings for the elderly and ailing President, Sir Martin Archer Shee. He was also on the hanging committee. However, he too was ill, and succumbing to strain. On 4th May, after the Academy dinner, he wrote to John Murray that he felt 'the sad necessity' of leaving London the next morning, and by the 15th he told John James Ruskin that 'really I have been so unwell that I was obliged to go away from Town to revival by a little change of fresh air'. In fact he had gone to Margate, and after resting for a few days, had crossed the Channel to Boulogne. From this short excursion come the first certainly dated or identifiable drawings of the year, those in the 'Ambleteuse and Wimereux' and 'Boulogne' sketchbooks (Cat. 11-17 & 18).

Three sheets from the former, including Cat. 11 (fig. 1) and 12, are dated 12 May. Fourteen drawings survive from this roll sketchbook, all but one being in watercolours. They record, with great immediacy, stormy spring clouds, the rising and setting sun, and showers over the coast, mostly if not always on the French shore near Calais. The final drawing, originally inside the back cover (Cat. 17), is an impression of a steamer obscured by mist or spray beyond the trough of a wave. It is remarkably close to the conception of 'Folkestone', and Turner's pictorial imagination was certainly at work in a single scene of a stranded whale, a warmly coloured and quite worked up study inscribed *I shall use this* (Cat. 13). The fusion of whaling imagery with Turner's Channel and Kent coast drawings must be mentioned again. For the present it is sufficient to observe that this drawing, like several in this sketchbook, is quite resolved compositionally – and, it might be added, emotionally, the trapped whale evoking more dramatically the rather melancholy conno-

tations suggested by the lonely figure hurrying across the shore (Cat. 12) or the lowering storm clouds (Cat. 11, 15, 16; fig. 2) in other sheets. A meditative, withdrawn and silent atmosphere pervades most of these impressions of a deserted coastline.

The twenty four drawings in the 'Boulogne' book (Cat. 18), including one of Wimereux, are generally bolder and more freely washed with a very liquid brush over pencil indications. The motif of the lonely figure on the shore is again recurrent. Ruskin's description, 'coloured indications or ideas', aptly defines their degree of topographical content or precision. But here too are studies of pure coast scenery, of the empty beaches and dramatic skies that are the themes of the smaller 'Channel' book (Cat. 8, pls. 2) that was probably first used on the same spring crossing and drawn in at other times during the summer, when Turner was back in England.

Turner had intended to visit Switzerland this year, but in June, following Shee's resignation as PRA, he was appointed Deputy President of the Academy and his duties kept him much at home. Moreover, his health was slow to improve and in fact he would never properly recover after 1845. He probably spent some further periods in Kent, whenever he could get away, but planned no more ambitious travels than a further excursion to France. It would be his last trip abroad.

In September Turner visited Dieppe and wandered along the coast of Picardy, 'as he said himself, looking out for storms and shipwrecks: he carried nothing with him but a change of linen and his sketchbook'. At Eu, continued the Redgrave brothers, he needed his shoes repaired, and took lodgings in a fisherman's house whence he was summoned one day to dine with King Louis-Philippe, at his chateau overlooking the town. After his landlady had cut up some of her linen to provide a fresh neck-cloth, Turner 'spent one of the pleasantest of evenings in chat with his old Twickenham acquaintance'.[8]

Turner may well have had a more particular purpose in visiting Eu at this time. The previous year he had been to Portsmouth to witness the arrival of the French king on a visit to England, and now he was perhaps intending to watch the return visit of Queen Victoria and the Prince

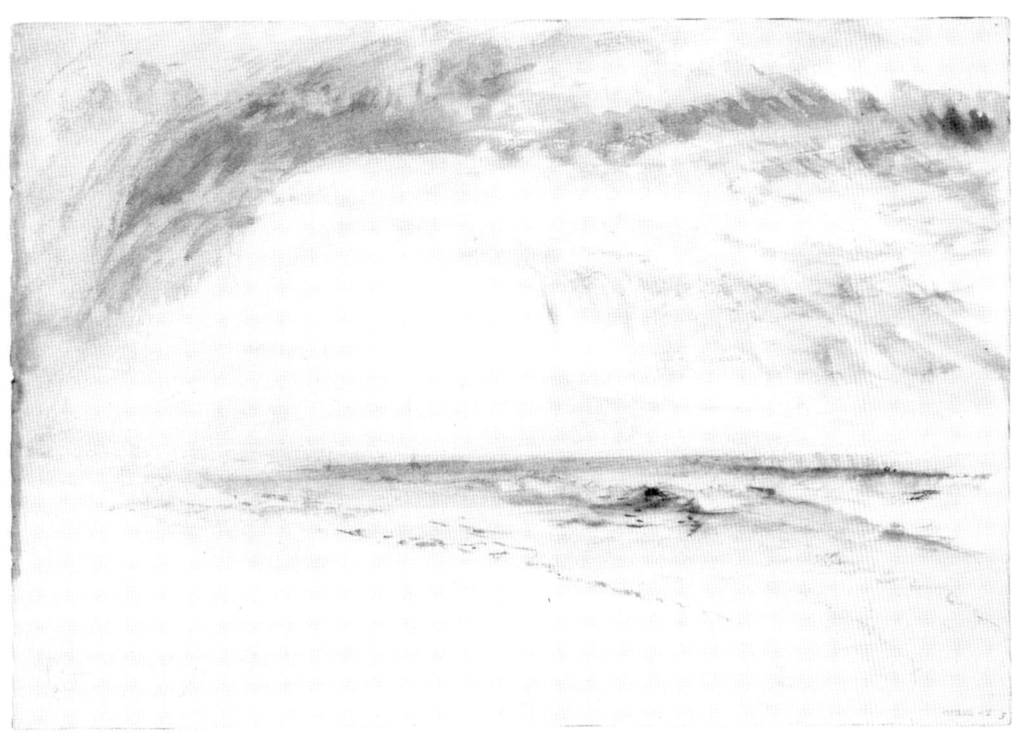

fig.1 **A Storm clearing up** 1845 (cat.11)

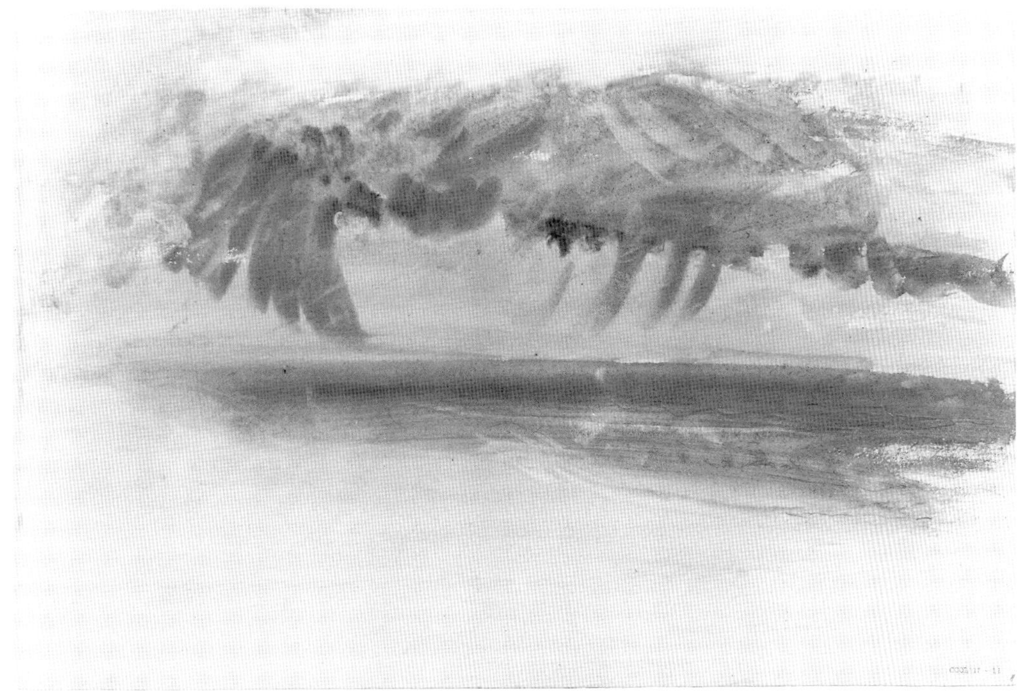

fig.2 **Storm Clouds, looking out to Sea** 1845 (cat.15)

Consort, for on 8 September the couple arrived at Tréport on the royal yacht and were entertained at a banquet in the chateau. Even if he did not attend this dinner, Turner could have imagined it in four sheets in one of the sketchbooks he used on this trip, the 'Dieppe' (Cat. 22); these show sumptuous candlelit banquets and entertainments, but in the absence of dates or inscriptions, their subjects cannot be certain.[9]

The Eu and Tréport subjects have a sketchbook to themselves, although this was broken up and the leaves distributed so that the contents, as listed by Finberg, are conjectural in a few cases. While still hastily drawn, these views are rather more finished than the majority of the late channel subjects, combining striking topographical effects of the royal chateau (Cat. 20, fig. 3) or the church at Tréport (Cat. 21) set high above the harbour and the town, with evocations of atmosphere as suggestive as any in the late Venetian or Swiss watercolours; the washes, moreover, are sometimes heightened with Turner's characteristic red ink to define architecture or details like the hussars in the foreground of Cat. 20. It is hard to believe that, in bringing these of all his last Channel coast subjects so far towards completion, Turner was not thinking of the possible capital to be made from watercolours of a place visited by the Queen, and his acquaintance with Louis Philippe, now apparently renewed, must also have been a factor. Certainly Ruskin recognized their outstanding qualities by including two of the views of the chateau, including Cat. 20, among his 'First Hundred' Turner drawings, in a trial exhibition for the National Gallery in 1857 that documented an imaginary continental tour beginning at Tréport itself.

The 'Dieppe' sketchbook from this autumn trip remains intact (Cat. 22), and contains twenty four drawings of the town and its harbour. Some are in watercolour over pencil, some in limpid pure watercolour. The harbour scenes, of which one is exhibited, are loosely worked up in speckled washes in the same manner as some of the less finished sheets in the 'Eu and Tréport' book. A delicate palette is used in most sheets although ff.4 and 5 employ only browns and ochres, and a hotter reddish orange range is, appropriately, the medium for the four banquet scenes at the end of the book (ff.20-24v.). The dramatic skies of the 'Ambleteuse and Wimereux', 'Boulogne' and 'Channel' books are less in evidence here, Turner's main focus being on urban or populous subjects, but on ff.15 and 16 are studies, in more sombre washes, of stormy marine views no less atmospheric than in the other books of 1845.

At the same time, and perhaps for longer periods this year, Turner was making pencil memoranda in the smaller 'Dieppe and Kent' book (cat. 23) which, as its title implies, ranges back and forth across the Channel. The first of these 'Scrawls at Dieppe', as Ruskin too dismissively called them, a sketch of figures at an apple stall, is dated *Sept. 11, 1845*, and this date recurs on an interior scene later in the book (f.78v.). These annotations are the main clues to the timing of Turner's visit, but although the first sketch is clearly French, there is nothing to indicate where it was made. This book contains a little map, with Eu and Tréport marked (f.69). Otherwise it is devoted to slight sketches of coastline, ships and steamers and scenes in a town, perhaps Dieppe itself, often several to a page and annotated with colour notes. Some pencil records of skies are broken into areas of colour and inscribed with colour notes (ie. f.107v.). In books like this were gathered the raw materials, the first impressions, of the subjects Turner developed in colour in the larger roll sketchbooks that he also took with him, and the colour studies in these are as likely to be imaginary, or recollected, as they are to be taken from nature. The correspondences noted by Finberg between pencil sketches in 'Dieppe and Kent' (ie. ff.2v. and 6), and subjects treated in watercolour in the so-called 'Ideas of Folkstone' book (cat. 24) (ie. ff.3 and 13), need not be coincidental, for Turner was still thinking pictorially, and gathering information to a purpose. He remained, as ever, totally professional.

'Ideas of Folkstone' was probably Turner's own title for this roll sketchbook (Cat. 24). Between two very liquid studies of stormy waters beating against a pier on the backs of the covers, it contains twenty three drawings of placid scenes around the town, some in watercolour over pencil and others in pure watercolour like the exhibited view of Folkestone harbour with a breakwater and a kind of pile-driving machine. Three studies

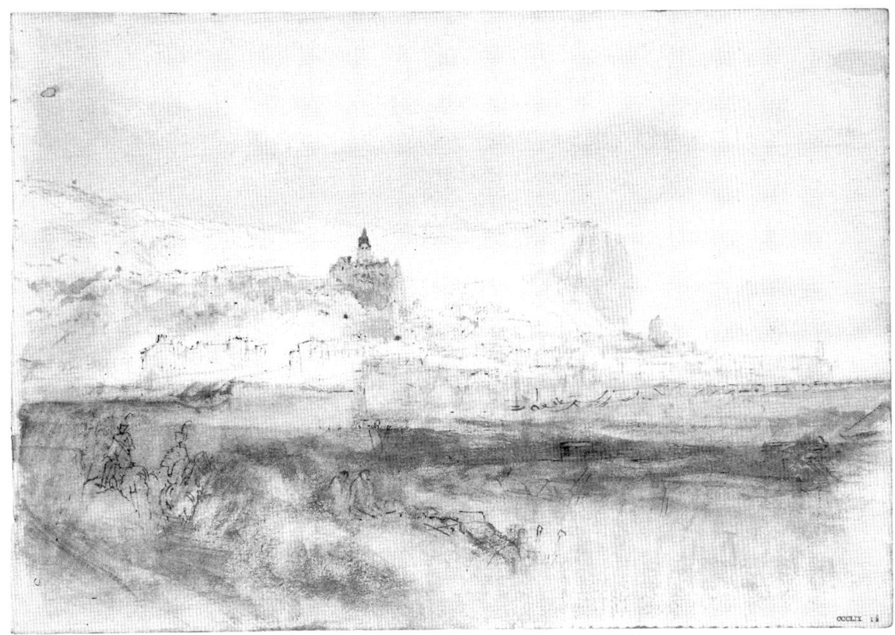

of skies and empty sands (ff.17-19), and especially
the latter two, are close to the subjects and senti-
ment of the 'Ambleteuse and Wimereux' book.
When Turner was in Folkestone in 1845 cannot
be certain, but it is most likely to have been in the
late summer or early autumn. The sketchbooks
give away no information, and may in any case
have been used simultaneously and drawn in at
different times during the year.

The 'Channel' Sketchbook and other related Work

All the main interests of Turner's 1845 sketches
recur, in colour but on a smaller scale than in the
roll sketchbooks, in the 'Channel' book (cat. 8,
pls. 2-5). Formerly in the possession of Mrs Booth
and of her son, this appeared on the London art
market in 1986. It had been acquired by the ven-
dor's family in the 1880s together with other
works by Turner, including an album of sketches,
mostly Kentish and continental scribbles on coloured paper, very feeble and obviously late in
date. If the latter drawings, already sold in 1978,
are by Turner, they must be of his dotage. The

sketchbook, on the other hand, is of great beauty
and highly important as the only known book of
later watercolours to have remained intact outside the Bequest.

Andrew Wilton, in a full discussion of the book,
has already noted its relationship to the documented work of 1845.[10] The eighty eight pages
bear seventy four sketches in colour and a small
group of sky studies in pencil, inscribed with colour notes, two of which (f.3 and f.14v.) are dated,
June 9 and *July 24*. Perhaps the watercolours were
done first, during Turner's May trip to Kent and
Boulogne, and the pencil sketches later, during
summer visits out of London. The topographical
locations are hardly ever distinct, and never made
explicit, although there is at least one sketch (f.
27v.) that is perhaps of Turner's familiar Margate
view, and there are others (ie. f.9) that show a
domed tower rather reminiscent of the cathedral
at Boulogne.

The majority of the sketches are taken looking
out to sea and are notable for their economy of
vision and execution. Sunsets, stormy skies and
rainclouds, wet sands at low tide, breaking waves,
ships in storms or mists on the horizon are caught
in rapid, very liquid washes, dragged in horizontal sweeps, smudged, or dashed in outbursts of

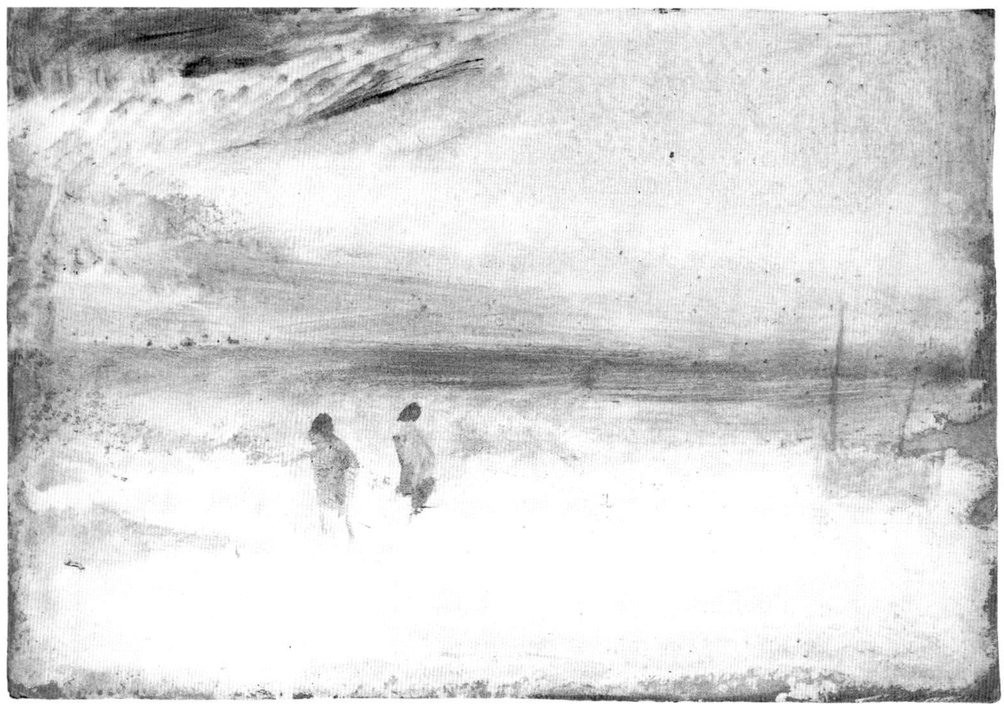

fig.4 **Two Figures on a Beach with a Boat** *c*.1840 (cat.4)

contending curves. Among all these impressions, familiar themes recur, especially the solitary, beachcombing figures, and small boats poised on empty waters. No other sketchbook so clearly anticipates the pictorial language of some groups of larger watercolours and sketches in the Bequest in which Turner addressed himself to the same subjects. Even if the relationships are only coincidental, they can only confirm a tendency towards abstraction in Turner's art at this period. Formal analysis of these late marine images will inevitably fall into all the clichés of Turner appreciation – reduction to horizontal planes of pure colour, distillation of form to simple masses defined against light – but it should be added that these characteristics are here exceptionally pronounced.

Certain leaves in the sketchbook can be matched closely elsewhere. For example f.24v., bearing a limpid sketch of two small, mist-shrouded sails at sea, may be compared to a separate watercolour (CCCLXIV.82) and to the oil sketch on millboard that must be of around the same date (Cat. 5), in both of which the focal

image is located against an almost blank field of colour. The oil belongs to a group of small sketches on board (Butlin and Joll 485-500), of which four are exhibited (Cat. 4-7; fig. 4). All have strong affinities with the 'Channel' book, although some have been tentatively dated up to a decade earlier. Similar motifs and execution may also be found in a series of quite large watercolours of coastal subjects. Of the six exhibited (Cat. 37-42) two show a comparably broad and fluent treatment of breaking waves, figures and distant ships (Cat. 39 and 42; fig. 6) that is clearly a later development of the manner used in the wave studies of the 1830s (Cat. 30 and 31). Others maintain the specific interest in skies and cloud formation, two, evidently drawn in quick succession, recording the progress of a storm shower over the shore (Cat. 40, fig. 5, and 41). Skies are treated in similar palette and handling in the 'Ambleteuse and Wimereux', 'Boulogne' and 'Dieppe' books, and in a number of separate sheets (Cat. 32-34), some of which bear late watermarks and which it would be pleasant to

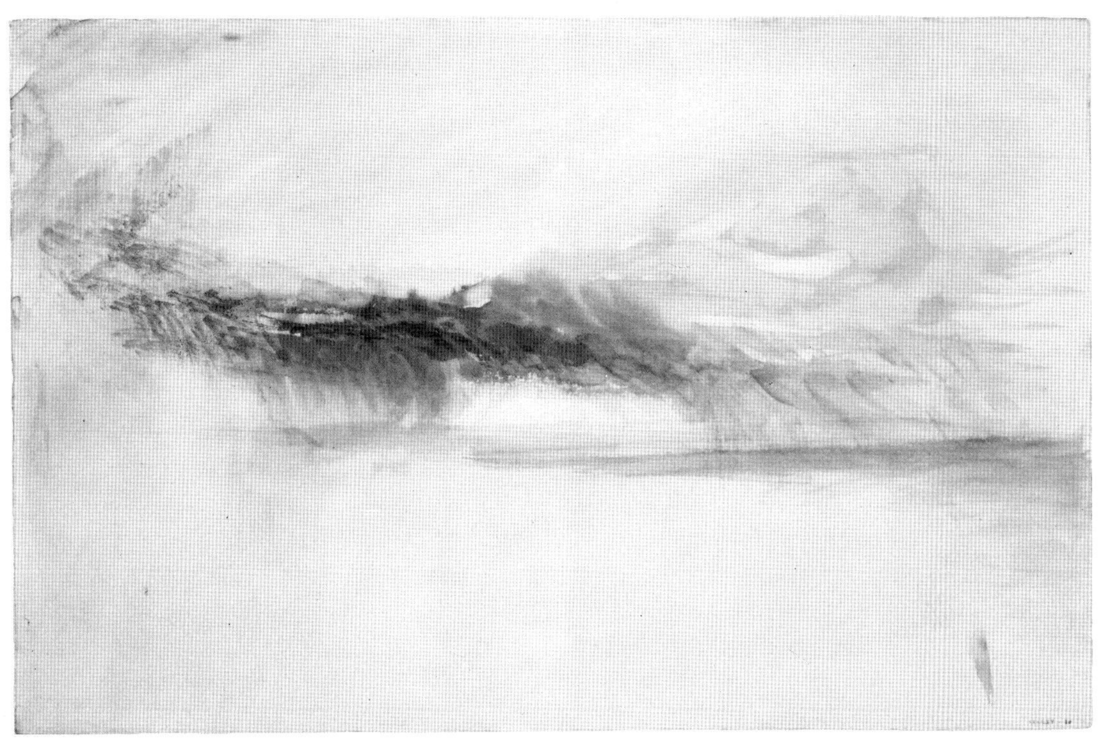

fig.5 **Rain Clouds** *c.*1843–5 (cat.40)

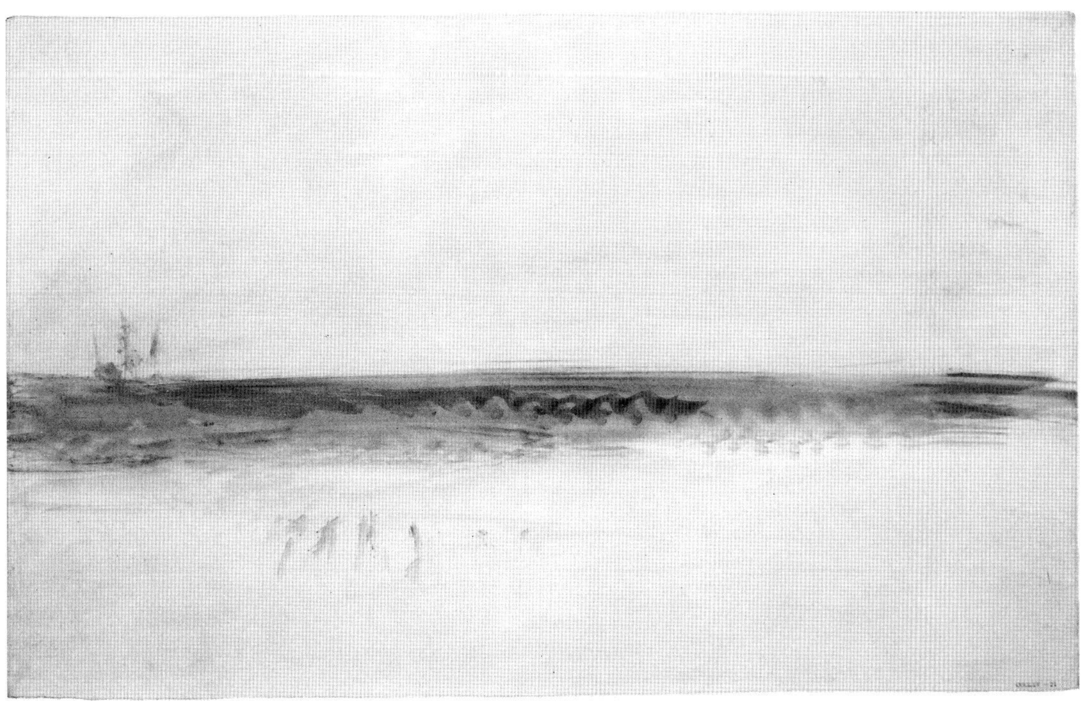

fig.6 **Blue Sea and distant Ship** *c.*1843–5 (cat.42)

think were drawn in Thanet from the 'loveliest skies in Europe'.

Normally one would be extremely cautious in drawing any such analogies, but the existence of significant numbers of directly comparable works, loose and unidentified in the Bequest and dispersed elsewhere, would paradoxically tend to confirm their integrity as a group of late date, and associated with Margate or Mrs Booth. For it was precisely these late drawings, slight, unfinished and highly personal, that were plundered from the studio after Turner's death, or, having been acquired by Mrs Booth, were given away by her or sold. The Bequest contains but the residue of the most vulnerable of all Turner's work after Ruskin, Charles Stokes and others had taken their pick. Thus, nineteen sheets of skies, seas and sands, grouped together by Wilton in 1979, may be added to the late Channel group.[11] They include the watercolour of a whaling subject, inscribed *He breaks away*, in the Fitzwilliam Museum, Cambridge, which on comparison of size and handling is most likely to be the single sheet missing from the 'Ambleteuse and Wimereux' book; the study probably of Margate pier in the Museum of Fine Arts, Boston; and the two drawings of wrecks, with rough poetic inscriptions linking their subjects to Turner's old theme of fallacious Hope, in the Yale Center for British Art and another American collection.

It was in 1851, the year of Turner's death, that Matthew Arnold first heard on Dover beach that 'melancholy, long, withdrawing roar'. The sad inevitability of the cycle of the seas was no less central to Turner's tragic sense. Although his own attempt to define it poetically – 'The refluent wave fell sluggish on the beach' – was too conventional, it occurred, in the 'Kent' sketchbook that Finberg thought was his last but is in fact almost certainly of some years earlier (Cat. 10), alongside a sketch of the doomed lovers Hero and Leander looking out across the water.[12] As his strength ebbed, and the Channel became his own uncrossable Hellespont, Turner allowed his imagination to play freely over its shores. In some late drawings like the Yale *Wreck* or the study of sea under low sun that he had drawn in the 'Ambleteuse and Wimereux' book (Cat. 14), his message is completely intrinsic, text or poetry being woven into

the very fabric of the design so that it is hardly distinguishable from the drawing itself. Elsewhere, he projected his imagination more deliberately, building up layer upon layer of meaning. Even so, however dense a tissue of allusion he spun around two of the pictures he prepared for exhibition in 1846, 'Undine giving the Ring to Massaniello, Fisherman of Naples' (Butlin & Joll 424) and 'The Angel standing in the Sun' (Butlin & Joll 425), we might recognize in their settings the glistening sands, scattered with marine life, that he had so often walked the previous summer. He had enjoyed studying the fish caught at Margate and around the coast (Cat. 28), and these too entered his fantasy whether in the grotesque form of the *Sea Monsters* (Cat. 3) or in the whales and other creatures that inhabit the waters in drawings like Cat. 27 (fig. 8).

Whales were already on Turner's mind. He had shown two whaling subjects, those in the Bequest (Butlin & Joll 414) and the Metropolitan Museum, New York (Butlin & Joll 415), in the Academy in 1845, both with references to Thomas Beale's *Natural History of the Sperm Whale*, and two others, *Hurrah! for the Whaler Erebus! another Fish!* (Butlin & Joll 423) and *Whalers (boiling Blubber)* (Butlin & Joll 426), both in the Bequest, were exhibited the following year. The 'Whalers' sketchbook, with its twenty drawings in chalks and watercolours of fish, figures, and marine and whaling compositions, was probably also used in 1845. Three sheets are exhibited (Cat. 26-28). The techniques used here are unusual for this period, the free use of chalks, and the preparation of the leaves with grey wash being more characteristic of Turner's practice in the previous decade. As Luke Herrmann has already observed, a spirited study of a steamer leaving harbour (Cat. 26, fig. 7) has every appearance of having been drawn from nature;[13] and the scene bears a strong resemblance to the harbour at Dieppe. Moreover, this sheet has greater technical integrity, being drawn entirely in chalks over the washed ground, and this is also the case in a further sheet from this book (Cat. 27, fig. 8). Others, however, appear to be hybrid works in which additions in chalk have been added to earlier drawings of coast scenes similar to the Margate sheets reassembled by Yardley. What could be

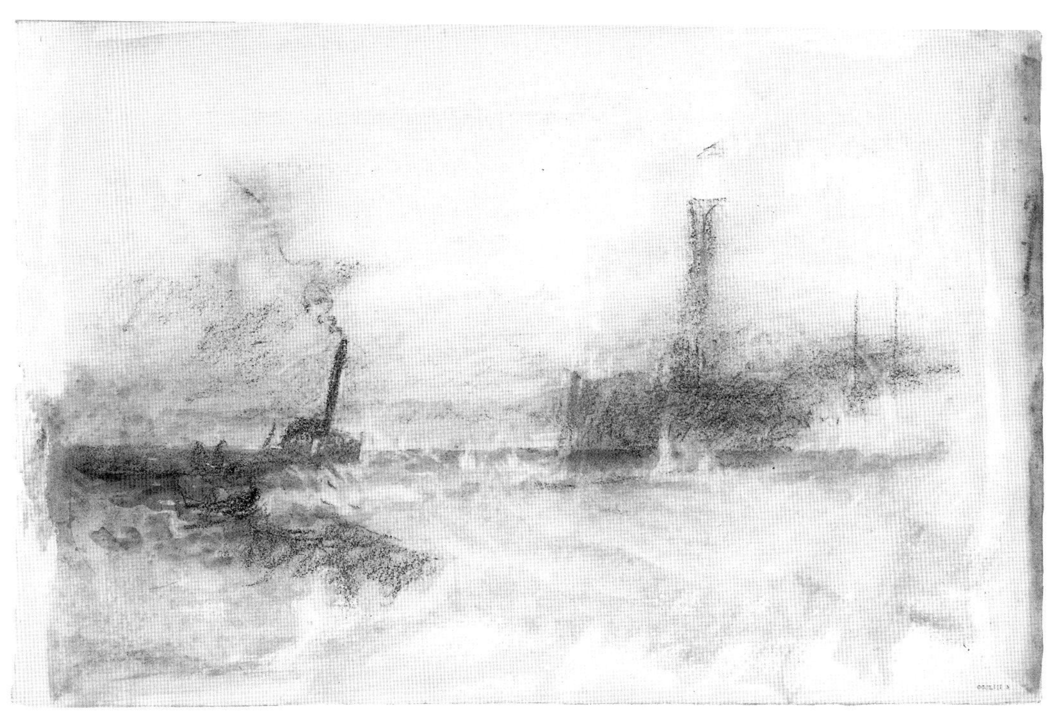

fig.7 **A Steamer leaving Harbour** *c.*1844–5 (cat.26)

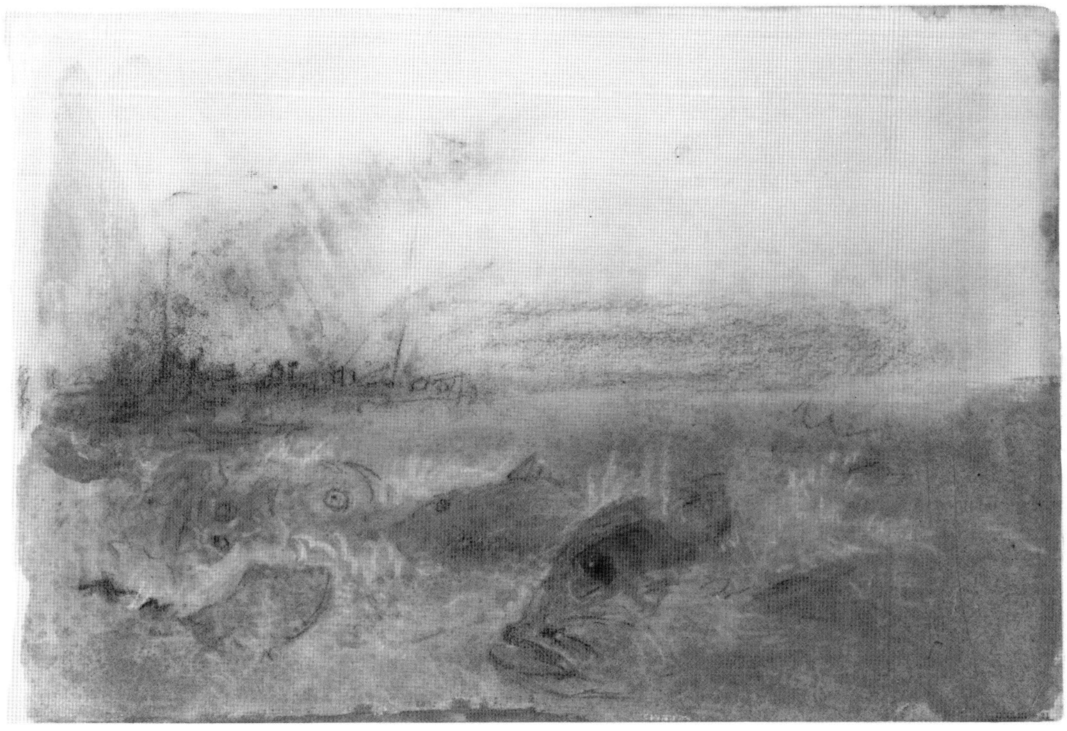

fig.8 **Tunny Fishing** *c.*1844–5 (cat.27)

more likely than that Turner worked over some earlier drawings, adding imaginary ideas on the whaling theme that, as we know from the (significantly very different) sketch in 'Ambleteuse and Wimereux', he was brooding in 1845? It is easy to guess the excitement of the subject for an artist so long devoted to subjects of the sea, and its imaginative appeal to a man for whom these were now to become a matter of meditation, and no longer of experience.

After his autumn trip in 1845, Turner never again left England. The following autumn or thereabouts, he moved Mrs Booth to Chelsea, to the banks of the Thames. At seventy-one, his horizons were fast narrowing. He did not, however, quite sever his connections with Margate, for he seems to have spent one last summer there in 1847. The little 'Hythe and Walmer' and 'Folkestone?' sketchbooks (CCCLV, and Cat. 25) perhaps contain his impressions. The former has fourteen leaves, some blue and others white, very perfunctorily drawn in pencil or chalks; the coastline is sometimes sketched as if from the water, indicating that Turner was still making short excursions by boat. The sheets in the latter book associated with Folkestone are in most cases hardly touched, and the hand is distinctly shaky. However, there are several sketches of large fully rigged ships or yachts dressed with bunting (ie. ff.12, 23v., 31 and 31v.) that suggest some kind of regatta and are interesting to compare with a group of watercolours of almost Oriental minimalism that it is tempting to place among Turner's very last, and most finely distilled, records of Kentish or Channel harbours.

Six sheets of this type are exhibited (Cat. 44-49). All show harbour scenes, often with ships dressed with flags and bunting. There is a sketch of a steamer moored alongside a quay (Cat. 46, fig. 9) and in only one example, that showing boats being rowed out in choppy waters (Cat. 45), is the mood other than calm. These drawings are, probably, impossible to date or place on internal evidence. In view of their rather festive air they might perhaps be associated with events like Louis-Philippe's arrival at Portsmouth in 1844, or the return visit of Victoria and Albert to Tréport in 1845; Cat. 44 in particular shows a vessel like a royal yacht. All that can be said is that the harbours seem quite extensive, while the arguments for a very late date are purely stylistic, there being little else to compare with these drawings unless it is that of a steamer off a small pier (Cat. 43 fig. 10), but this is probably Margate and a little earlier.

The execution of this group of drawings is both rudimentary and highly descriptive. The paper is left widely exposed, and only the briefest of pencil notes are suggested, but hints of wash in pellucid pastels – blues, greys, browns and coral pinks – are dotted and dabbed to define masts, flags, a line of coast or a building. If we are reminded of calligraphy, we may well sense the handwriting of an old man – but one still imaginative and professional enough to muster his diminished resources to the best possible effect.

David Blayney Brown

NOTES

[1] M. Butlin and E. Joll, *The Paintings of J.M.W. Turner*, revised ed., 1984, I, pp.288-9, No.472.

[2] John Pound's pictures were sold at Christie's, 25 March 1865.

[3] W. Thornbury, *The Life of J.M.W. Turner R.A.*, 1862, I, pp.25.

[4] Repr. A. Wilton, *Turner in his Time*, 1987, p.18, fig.17.

[5] Ruskin, Letter 9 (September 1871), *Fors Clavigera*, I, in E.T. Cook and A. Wedderburn, *Works of John Ruskin*, 1907, XXVII, pp.161-4.

[6] For a photograph of Margate with Mrs Booth's house marked, see B. Falk, *Turner the Painter; his Hidden Life*, 1938, facing p.206. Falk claims that Turner removed Mrs Booth to Deal, further to protect their privacy.

[7] E. Yardley, 'A Margate Sketchbook Re-assembled?', *Turner Studies*, Vol.4, No.2, Winter 1984, pp.53-5.

[8] R. and S. Redgrave, *A Century of Painters of the British School*, 1866, II, p.86.

[9] On the royal visit to Eu and Tréport, see G. Finley, 'Turner, the Apocalypse and History: "The Angel" and "Undine"', *Burlington Magazine*, CXXI, 1979, pp.685-95.

[10] A. Wilton, 'A Rediscovered Turner Sketchbook', *Turner Studies*, Vol.6, No.2, Winter 1986, pp.9-23.

[11] A. Wilton, *The Life and Work of J.M.W. Turner*, 1979, pp.469-71, Nos.1411-29 repr.

[12] TB CCCLXIII, 28a-29.

[13] L. Herrmann, 'Turner and the Sea', *Turner Studies*, Vol.1, No.1, Winter 1980, pp.15-6.

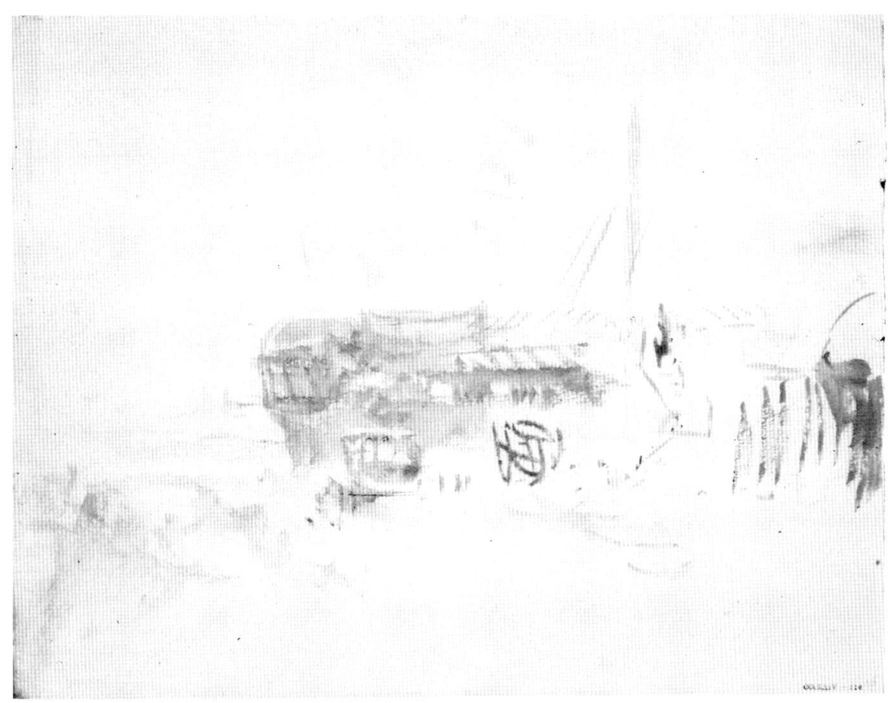

fig.9 **A Ship moored at a Quay** *c*.1845 (cat.46)

fig.10 **A Steamer off a Pier,? Margate** *c*.1843 (cat.43)

List of Exhibits

PAINTINGS

1 **Seascape: Folkestone** *c.*1845
Canvas $34\frac{3}{4} \times 46\frac{1}{4}$ (88.3 × 117.5)
Butlin and Joll 472
Private Collection (pl.1)

2 **Rough Sea** *c.*1840-45
Canvas 36×48 (91.5 × 122)
Butlin and Joll 471
TG 5479

3 **Sunrise with Sea Monsters** *c.*1845
Canvas 36×48 (91.5 × 122)
Butlin and Joll 473
TG 1990

4 **Two Figures on a Beach with a
Boat** *c.*1840-45
Millboard, irregular $9\frac{5}{8} \times 13\frac{5}{8}$ (24.5 × 34.5)
TG D36681 (fig.4)

5 **Sailing Boat in a rough Sea** *c.*1840-45
Millboard, irregular $10\frac{1}{2} \times 11\frac{15}{16}$ (26.5 × 30.5)
TG D36677

6 **Shore Scene with Waves and
Breakwater** *c.*1835?
Millboard, irregular 9×12 (23 × 30.5)
TG D36680

7 **Figures on a Beach** *c.*1840-45
Millboard, irregular $10\frac{3}{16} \times 11\frac{3}{4}$ (26 × 30)
TG D36690

SKETCHBOOKS

8 **'Channel' Sketchbook** *c.*1845
Page size $3\frac{3}{4} \times 6\frac{5}{16}$ (95 × 162)
f.67v.; **A Ship at Sea in misty Weather**
watercolour, drawn upside down
Private Collection (pls 2-5)

9 **'Gravesend and Margate'
Sketchbook** *c.*1832
Page size $8\frac{1}{8} \times 3\frac{3}{8}$ (208 × 83)
ff.30v.,31; **Custom House and Jetty at
Margate, and Cliffs** pencil
TB CCLXXIX: TG D27322/D27323

10 **Kent Sketchbook** ?1830s
Page size $3 \times 3\frac{7}{8}$ (75 × 98)
f.27; **'Pegwell Bay'; Sandwich; Clouds;
Figures aboard a Packet Boat:** inscribed
Cuyp, pencil
TB CCCLXIII: TG D35806

11-17, from the **Ambleteuse and Wimereux
Sketchbook** 1845
Page size $9\frac{3}{8} \times 13\frac{1}{4}$ (287 × 335)
TB CCCLVII

11 (f.3) **A Storm clearing up** dated *12 May,
45*, watercolour over pencil
TG D35388 (fig.1)

12 (f.5) **Figures on the Shore** dated *12 May,
45*, watercolour over pencil
TG D35390

13 (f.6) **Looking out to Sea; a Whale
stranded** inscribed *I shall use* (?) *this*,
watercolour over pencil
TG D35391

14 (f.7) **Sun over Water** illegibly inscribed in
the waves, watercolour over pencil
TG D35392

15 (f.11) **Storm Clouds, looking out to Sea**
watercolour over pencil
TG D35397 (fig.2)

16 (f.12) **Storm Clouds, looking out to Sea**
watercolour over pencil
TG D35399

17 (f.14; inside back cover) **A Shower over the Sea** watercolour over pencil
TG D35401

18 **Boulogne Sketchbook** 1845
Page size $9\frac{1}{16} \times 12\frac{3}{4}$ (231 × 323)
f.6; **Storm approaching** watercolour over pencil
TB CCCLVIII: TG D35408

19-21, from the **Eu and Tréport Sketchbook** 1845
Page size $9\frac{1}{16} \times 12\frac{3}{4}$ (231 × 323)
TB CCCLIX

19 (f.3) **Cliffs on Coast, with a Tower** watercolour over pencil
TG D35438

20 (f.12) **Eu, with Louis Philippe's Chateau** watercolour and ink over pencil
TG D35447   (fig.3)

21 (f.17) **Tréport** watercolour over pencil
TG D35452

22 **Dieppe Sketchbook** 1845
Page size $9\frac{1}{8} \times 12\frac{15}{16}$ (232 × 329)
f.6; **A sunny Day at Dieppe** watercolour over pencil
TB CCCLX: TG D35464

23 **Dieppe and Kent Sketchbook** 1845
Page size $3\frac{3}{8} \times 4\frac{7}{16}$ (86 × 113)
ff.23v., 24; **A Fishing Village on a rocky Coast** pencil
TB CCCLXI; TG D35528/D35529

24 'Ideas of Folkstone' **Sketchbook** 1845
Page size $9\frac{1}{16} \times 12\frac{7}{8}$ (230 × 327)
f.4; **The Harbour** watercolours
TB CCCLVI: TG D35364

25 **Folkestone (?) Sketchbook** ? 1847
Page size $2\frac{15}{16} \times 4\frac{7}{16}$ (75 × 113)
f.8; **View of Coast with Boats** pencil
TB CCCLXII: TG D35698

26-28, from the **Whalers Sketchbook** c.1844-5
Page size $8\frac{3}{4} \times 13$ (221 × 332)
TB CCCLIII

26 (f.5) **A Steamer leaving Harbour** black and white chalks over grey preparation
TG D35244   (fig.7)

27 (f.3) **Tunny Fishing** red, black and white chalks over grey preparation
TG D35260   (fig.8)

28 (f.22) **Study of Fish** watercolour and bodycolour over grey preparation
TG D35261

OTHER DRAWINGS

29 **Harbour, Lighthouse and Jetty** c.1830
Black and white chalks and red bodycolour on blue paper $5\frac{1}{2} \times 7\frac{1}{2}$ (140 × 188)
TB CCXXIV 29: TG D20319

30 **Rain clouds over the Sea** ?c.1832
Bodycolour on blue paper $7\frac{1}{2} \times 11\frac{1}{4}$ (191 × 285)
TB CCCLXIV 411: TG 36279

31 **The Breaking Wave** ?c.1832
Bodycolour on blue paper $7\frac{5}{8} \times 11$ (193 × 279)
TB CCCLXIV 417: TG D36285

32 **A stormy Sky** ?1840-45
Watercolour $9\frac{1}{2} \times 12\frac{1}{2}$ (242 × 307)
TB CCCLXIV 35: D35874

33 **A stormy Sky** ?1840-45
Watercolour $9\frac{1}{2} \times 12$ (246 × 304)
TB CCCLXIV 36; TG D35875

34 **Storm Clouds** ?1845
Watercolour $8\frac{1}{2} \times 11$ (220 × 279)
Watermark: J. Whatman. 1841
TB CCCLXIV 38: TG D35877

35 **Choppy Waves**
Watercolour and bodycolour $9\frac{5}{8} \times 12$
(244×305)
TB CCCLXIV 62 : TG D35905

36 **Sea and Sky**
Watercolour $8\frac{1}{2} \times 10\frac{1}{2}$ (219×269)
TB CCCLXIV 78 : TG D35921

37 **A Storm** *c.*1843-5
Watercolour $11\frac{1}{2} \times 17\frac{1}{4}$ (291×437)
TB CCCLXV 10; TG D36300

38 **A Shore** *c.*1843-5
Watercolour $11\frac{1}{2} \times 17\frac{1}{4}$ (280×441)
TB CCCLXV 11; TG D36301

39 **On the Beach** *c.*1843-5
Watercolour $11\frac{1}{2} \times 17\frac{1}{4}$ (291×437)
TB CCCLXV 18; TG D36308

40 **Rain Clouds** *c.*1843-5
Watercolour $11\frac{1}{2} \times 17\frac{1}{4}$ (291×441)
TB CCCLXV 19; TG D36309   (fig.5)

41 **A stormy Sky** *c.*1843-5
Watercolour $11\frac{1}{2} \times 17\frac{1}{4}$ (289×438)
TB CCCLXV 20: TG D36310

42 **Blue Sea and distant Ship** *c.*1843-5
Watercolour $11\frac{1}{2} \times 17\frac{1}{4}$ (283×444)
TB CCCLXV 21: TG D36311   (fig.6)

43 **A Steamer off a Pier, ? Margate** *c.*1843
Watercolour $9\frac{1}{2} \times 11\frac{3}{4}$ (241×298)
Watermark: J. Whatman. 1841
TB CCCLXIV 173: TG D36017   (fig.10)

44 **Sailing Ship surrounded by small
Boats** *c.*1845
Watercolour $9\frac{1}{4} \times 12\frac{3}{8}$ (239×318)
TB CCCLXIV 138: TG D35981

45 **'Going out to the Ship – sculls
Rough'** *c.*1845
Watercolour over pencil $9\frac{1}{4} \times 12$ (236×311)
TB CCCLXIV 114: TG D35957

46 **A Ship moored at a Quay** *c.*1845
Watercolour $9 \times 11\frac{1}{2}$ (226×291)
TB CCCLXIV 116: TG D35959   (fig.9)

47 **A Harbour with Shipping** *c.*1845
Watercolour $9\frac{1}{4} \times 12\frac{1}{4}$ (241×311)
TB CCCLXIV 109: TG D35952

48 **A Harbour with Shipping** *c.*1845
Watercolour $9\frac{1}{4} \times 12\frac{1}{4}$ (239×315)
TB CCCLXIV 115: TG D35958

49 **A Harbour with Shipping** *c.*1845
Watercolour $9\frac{1}{4} \times 12\frac{1}{4}$ (237×312)
TB CCCLXIV 57: TG D35899

PRINT

Robert Wallis after Turner

50 **Margate, Kent** engraving, 1832, for
**Picturesque Views in England and
Wales**
$9\frac{5}{8} \times 6\frac{1}{4}$ (244×159)
Rawlinson 263 T04592